EINSTEIN
IN HIS OWN WORDS

EINSTEIN
IN HIS OWN WORDS

Anne Rooney

GRAMERCY BOOKS

NEW YORK

Published by Gramercy Books, an imprint of Random House Value Publishing, a division of Random House, Inc., New York, by arrangement with Arcturus Publishing Limited.

Anne Rooney has asserted her right to be identified as the author of this work under the Copyright, Design and Patents Act 1988

Gramercy is a registered trademark and the colophon is a trademark of Random House, Inc.

Random House
New York • Toronto • London • Sydney • Auckland
www.randomhouse.com

Printed and bound in Malaysia

Editor: Paul Whittle
Art Director: Beatriz Waller
Designer: Zeta Fitzpatrick

A catalog record for this title is available from the Library of Congress.

ISBN-13: 978-0-517-22847-0
ISBN-10: 0-517-22847-5

10 9 8 7 6 5 4 3 2 1

CONTENTS

INTRODUCTION 6

SCIENCE 32

RELIGION 104

WAR 130

POLITICS 158

PHILOSOPHY 170

WHO'S WHO 188

CREDITS 192

INTRODUCTION:

GENIUS
AND ICON

'In the past it never occurred to me that every casual remark of mine would be snatched up and recorded. Otherwise I would have crept further into my shell.'

In the last hundred years, the name 'Albert Einstein' has become shorthand for 'genius'. He ranks alongside Isaac Newton and Leonardo da Vinci as one of the greatest thinkers of all time. His face, with its unruly halo of hair and its comic moustache, is universally recognized, even though few people fully understand his work.

'Does it make a silly impression on me, that excitement of crowds, here and yonder, about my theories of which they cannot understand a word? I think it is funny and also interesting to observe. I am sure that it is the mystery of non-understanding that appeals to them… it impresses them, it has the color and the appeal of the mysterious… and one becomes enthusiastic and gets excited.'

Memorial plaque to Einstein in his home town of Ulm

How did a part-time scientist, exploring an area of physics incomprehensible to most people, become so iconic a figure?

'Let me… tell you what I look like: pale face, long hair, and a tiny beginning of a paunch. In addition an awkward gait, and a cigar in the mouth — if he happens to have a cigar — and a pen in his pocket or his hand. But crooked legs and warts he does not have, and so he is quite handsome — also no hair on his hands such as is often found on ugly men.'

With his wild hair and unkempt clothes Einstein was hardly glamorous. Yet his eccentric appearance, coupled with his honesty, humility and willingness to pronounce on almost any topic, captured and held the imagination of the public in Europe and the USA. Here was a man of undoubted intellectual stature who would reply to letters from school children; a man who advised world leaders yet couldn't — or wouldn't — find a clean shirt and a pair of socks. It was an endearing image.

Several other aspects of Einstein's story and character contributed to his appeal. He was the epitome of the 'small man made good'. While working as a patent clerk in Switzerland, with no university affiliation, Einstein produced some of the most important scientific papers ever published, overturning the world view that had endured since Newton's time. And yet he never became arrogant or presented himself as other than an ordinary person.

'Let every man be respected as an individual and no man be idolized.'

Furthermore, he was honest, courageous and undaunted by the social standing or formal authority of others. He stood up for what he believed in and spoke out with no regard for any trouble his actions might cause him.

Einstein's enthusiasm — his real passion for science and the universe it defined — was, and remains, inspirational.

'Whoever… can no longer wonder, no longer marvel, is as good as dead, and his eyes are dimmed.'

'We never cease to stand like curious children before the great Mystery into which we are born.'

He wanted to share the wonders he had discovered. He wrote an explanation of relativity for *The Times* so that everyone, not just trained physicists and the readers of academic journals, might be able to grasp the new shape of science. He felt strongly that science must be explained in terms that ordinary people could understand.

'Out yonder there was this huge world, which exists independently of us human beings and which stands before us like a great, eternal riddle, at least partially accessible to our inspection and thinking. The contemplation of this world beckoned like a liberation, and I soon noticed that many a man I had learned to esteem and admire had found inner freedom and security in devoted occupation with it.'

Despite his best intentions, ordinary people have not found it easy to understand his science. Einstein's field, theoretical physics, is as mysterious as alchemy to most people. His most famous equation, $E=mc^2$, is more often recited like a spell than it is understood. Even so, even amongst those who don't really understand what it was, there is universal recognition that his achievement was world-changing.

100 JAHRE RELATIVITÄT – ATOME – QUANTEN

55

ALBERT EINSTEIN

$$E = mc^2$$

DEUTSCHLAND

2005

German stamp, commemorating the 100th anniversary of the Special Theory of Relativity

'Why is it that nobody understands me and everybody likes me?'

Einstein's key discoveries did more than change the face of science. They redefined the universe in a deeper way. The philosophical implications of his revelations about the nature of space and time overturned everything, recasting the nature of physical reality. Suddenly, there was no stable frame of reference. 'Here' and 'now' no longer had any simple meaning. Instead of time running unremittingly forwards at a steady pace it could be slowed, or perhaps hastened. In some circumstances, it might be stopped. A point in space could no longer be fixed, because everything moves. The new fusion of space and time — space-time — was his creation.

His former teacher, Hermann Minkowski, quickly absorbed these ideas.

'Henceforth space itself and time by itself are doomed to fade away into mere shadows, and only a kind of union of the two will preserve an independent reality.'

[Hermann Minkowski, 1908]

The early years

'My life is a simple thing that would interest no one. It is a known fact that I was born, and that is all that is necessary.'

Einstein as a child with his younger sister

'I was born, the son of Jewish parents, on 14 March 1879 in Ulm. My father was a merchant, moved shortly after my birth to Munich, in 1893 to Italy, where he remained till his death (1902). I have no brother, but a sister who lives in Italy.'

Einstein was no child prodigy. He records that his father even consulted a doctor because he was so late in learning to speak that his parents worried that he might be backward.

He did not take well to the authoritarian, even militaristic, nature of the *Gymnasium* — the German secondary school — which he was forced to attend. He made little attempt to fit in or do what was required of him, and later recalled a teacher saying of him

'Your mere presence here undermines the class's respect for me.'

This disdain for authority, and rules for which he could see no reason, continued throughout his life. It brought him trouble, but it contributed to his public appeal and it gave him the freedom to be true to his beliefs and to say what he pleased.

When the family's electrical engineering business failed in 1894, Einstein's parents and younger sister moved to Milan. The young Albert stayed at the Gymnasium, but did not stick with it for long.

'I am nothing but a burden to my family… Really, it would have been better if I had never been born.'

Early in the next year he followed them to Italy, leaving school before taking the baccalaureate exams that would have enabled him to go to university. Instead, he eventually went to the Polytechnic Institute in Zurich, Switzerland, in order to study engineering.

Einstein, seated, far left, with his graduation class at the Cantonal School, Aarau

'I too, was originally supposed to become an engineer. But I found the idea intolerable of having to apply the inventive faculty to matters that make everyday life even more elaborate — and all, just for dreary money-making.'

'If I would be a young man again and had to decide how to make my living, I would not try to become a scientist or scholar or teacher. I would rather choose to be a plumber or a peddler, in the hope of finding that modest degree of independence still available under present circumstances.'

In 1896 he gave up his German citizenship, so avoiding military service, and remained stateless for five years. He was later to declare repeatedly that he considered military service to be one of the worst abuses the state can inflict on the individual.

Einstein with Mileva

While at the Polytechnic, Einstein met and fell in love with the woman who was to become his first wife, the Serbian Mileva Marič.

'How was I ever able to live alone, my little everything? Without you I have no self-confidence, no passion for work, and no enjoyment of life — in short, without you, my life is a void.'

His family disapproved heartily of the alliance because Mileva was not only foreign and non-Jewish but was studying a subject not considered suitable for a woman. She was also older than Einstein and was disabled. 'You're ruining your future... no decent family would want her', his mother said of Mileva.

'My parents are very distressed about my love for you... My parents mourn for me almost as if I had died. Again and again they wail to me that I brought misfortune on myself by my promise to you... this is enough to drive one crazy!'

In 1901, Mileva became pregnant. She returned to her family to give birth, but it appears that their daughter Lieserl died very young for there are no references to her after 1903.

Einstein's father died in 1902, and he was finally able to marry Mileva. They had two further children, both boys, one of whom was later institutionalized because of mental illness.

'As a student he was treated contemptuously by the professors… he has no understanding of how to get on with important people.'

[*Friedrich Adler*]

Einstein (right) with colleagues at Bern

Einstein was disappointed not to be given a position at the Polytechnic after achieving his degree in 1900, and took a series of teaching and tutoring jobs before securing a post as Technical Expert, Third Class, at the Patent Office in Bern, Switzerland. His work at the patent office gave him the intellectual space to pursue his interest in physics and mathematics.

Physics above all

THEN, like Newton before him in 1665, he had an annus mirabilis. In 1905, he submitted his doctoral thesis and published three of his most important papers, including his first two statements of the special theory of relativity. The second of these included a form of the now-famous equation $E=mc^2$.

'The theory of relativity may indeed be said to have put a sort of finishing touch to the mighty intellectual edifice of Maxwell and Lorentz, inasmuch as it seeks to extend field physics to all phenomena... this theory is not speculative in origin; it owes its invention entirely to the desire to make physical theory fit observed facts as well as possible.'

Not everyone agreed with Einstein's conclusions. Opponents rejected and even ridiculed his special theory of relativity, and it took until 1908 for him to secure an academic appointment in Zurich.

Life with Mileva was difficult, partly because of her mental illness and partly because of Einstein's flirtations with other women — his cousin Elsa in particular. The couple began to separate soon after their arrival in Berlin in 1914, where Einstein had been appointed professor of theoretical physics.

'I treat my wife as an employee I cannot fire.'

It took five years before Mileva agreed to a divorce. After the divorce he only saw his sons on rare occasions, because Mileva discouraged contact.

'At the time we were separating from each other, the thought of leaving the children stabbed me like a dagger every morning when I awoke; I have never regretted the step in spite of it.'

Professionally, the separation was a productive period for Einstein, who was completing the general theory of relativity.

'No wonder that the love of science thrives under these circumstances, for it lifts me impersonally, and without railing

and wailing, from the vale of tears into peaceful spheres.'

Einstein finally married Elsa in 1919, soon after the divorce from Mileva was finalized, but not before he had complicated the issue by falling in love with Ilse, Elsa's daughter from her first marriage. He had even expressed interest in Elsa's younger sister, Paula.

The general theory of relativity made Einstein an overnight celebrity. Invited to speak and write everywhere, he was instantly popular, even with those who could understand little or none of his work.

Einstein was awarded the Nobel Prize in 1922, but it was for his work on light rather than the controversial work on relativity. Honouring an unusual clause of his divorce settlement, he sent the money to Mileva, keeping only the medal for himself.

Nobel prize winners 1933: Sinclair Lewis (Literature), Frank Billings Kellogg (Peace), Einstein and Irving Langmuir (Chemistry)

Persecution

POLITICALLY, though, life became increasingly difficult for Einstein. He suffered persecution as a Jew, even though he was a non-believer. During the early 1930s, Einstein became an enemy of the Nazis. He spoke out against them and his books were among those that were publicly burned. He was listed with other Jewish scientists whose work was denigrated and whom the National Socialist party wanted expunged from German science, and his photograph was printed with the caption 'not yet hanged'.

Above: *Nazis burn books, 1933, shortly after their assumption of power*

'Arrows of hate have been aimed at me too, but they have never hit me, because somehow they belonged to another world with which I have no connection whatsoever.'

The Nazis eventually seized Einstein's money. He was travelling at the time, and he returned to Belgium instead of Germany. He emigrated to the USA for good in 1933 and he never visited Germany again.

'[Germany] is like a man with a badly upset stomach who has not yet vomited enough.'

'I did not wish to live in a country where the individual does not enjoy equality before the law and freedom to say and teach what he likes.'

A new world

O UTSIDE Germany, the world welcomed him with open arms. Einstein was soon installed at the Institute for Advanced Study in Princeton, which he referred to as 'a banishment to paradise'. He was charmed by the reception he received. Although he was initially bemused by his fame and popularity, he reigned as a celebrity. In a letter to his friend Queen Elizabeth of Belgium, he described Princeton as:

Einstein with his second wife, Elsa

'A quaint ceremonious village of puny demigods on stilts.'

Elsa died in 1936, a blow that hit Einstein hard.

'I have got used extremely well to life here. I live like a bear in my den... The bearishness has been further enhanced by the death of my woman comrade, who was better with other people than I am.'

He adapted to his new life, and engaged increasingly in the political sphere, speaking and writing frequently on causes close to his heart. A reporter in *Time* magazine wrote in 1938 that:

'The Albert Einstein of today is no longer the timid bewildered man who visited the U.S. in 1930. He has acquired considerable poise in public, is not so afraid of the world as he used to be, entertains frequently. He has learned that it is not necessary to associate with anyone whom he does not like and trust.'

Einstein pledges allegiance at his US citizenship ceremony

After a while, Einstein became unpopular with the authorities in the USA, just as he had been in Germany, because of his refusal to toe the line and reserve comment on political matters. A Brooklyn newspaper wrote of his opposition to US policy with regard to the Spanish civil war:

'Professor Einstein at a time of personal peril was given sanctuary in this land.

Now he is engaged in telling our government how to run its business. This is sufficiently impertinent and arrogant… Someone might say: 'Wouldn't you think as long as this country took Einstein in out of the storm he would at least wait a few years before dictating to the government?'

'I have become a kind of *enfant terrible* in my new homeland because of my inability to keep silent and swallow everything that happens here.'

'The big political doings of our time are so disheartening that in our generation one feels quite alone. It is as if people had lost the passion for justice and dignity and no longer treasured what better generations had won by extraordinary sacrifices.'

Despite his involvement in politics and other areas, Einstein remained first and foremost a scientist. He spent his later life striving towards a unifying theory of everything, an explanation of the universe that would bind together general relativity, the behaviour of atoms and gravity. He battled with the champions of opposing theories — Niels Bohr, in particular — until the end of his life, and he continued working on his equations until his very last days.

'In the fundamental researches going on in physics we are in a state of groping, nobody having faith in what the other fellow is attempting with high hope. One lives all one's life under constant tension till it is time to go for good. But there remains for me the consolation that the essential part of my work has become part of the accepted basis of our science.'

Opposite: *Einstein with Chaim Weizmann (left) and New York mayor John F. Hyland (second from left)*

SCIENCE:

SCIENTIFIC

GENIUS

EINSTEIN is widely regarded as the greatest scientific genius of the last 300 years — and perhaps of all time. Yet although he engaged with some of the most complex and challenging ideas, he was convinced that any explanations of the workings of the universe should, in their essence, be simple and elegant.

'All physical theories… ought to lend themselves to so simple a description that even a child could understand them.'

Many people might discover beauty in a Beethoven symphony or a great painting — Einstein found it in a perfect theory or equation. His devotion to physics was passionate and all-consuming.

'I believe with Schopenhauer that one of the strongest motives that lead men to art and science is escape from everyday life with its painful crudity and hopeless dreariness, from the fetters of one's own ever-shifting desires.'

Einstein with model of the Hale telescope, Caltech, 1937

'The state of mind which enables a man to do work of this kind is akin to that of the religious worshipper or the lover; the daily effort comes from no deliberate intention or programme, but straight from the heart.'

Although his best and most revolutionary work was achieved in the first half of his life, Einstein's enthusiasm and dedication were undimmed by age. The physical world and the laws that govern it filled him with a sense of enduring wonder.

'As in my youth, I sit here endlessly and think and calculate, hoping to unearth deep secrets. The so-called Great World, i.e. men's bustle, has less attraction than ever, so that each day I find myself becoming more of a hermit.'

He was driven always by an overpowering desire to understand the universe, which led to his famous neglect of his own person. The archetypal image of the distracted scientist with messy hair and unkempt clothes has its origin in Einstein, too preoccupied with the work of genius to care whether he shaved or wore socks.

'If I were to start taking care of my grooming, I would no longer be my own self… So, to hell with it. If you find me so unappetizing, then look for a friend who is more palatable to female tastes.'

'I sold myself body and soul to Science — a flight from the 'I' and 'we' to the 'it'.'

That science was what drove his life is summed up in a comment made by a friend, Leopold Infeld:

'It seemed that the difference between life and death for Einstein consisted only in the difference between being able and not being able to do physics.'

The scientist's role

'The supreme task of the physicist is to arrive at those universal elementary laws from which the cosmos can be built up by pure deduction. There is no logical path to these laws; only intuition, resting on sympathetic understanding of experience, can reach them.'

'Scientific research can reduce superstition by encouraging people to think and survey things in terms of cause and effect.'

'Certain it is that a conviction, akin to religious feeling, of the rationality or intelligibility of the world lies behind all scientific work of a higher order.'

A cluster of galaxies makes a gravity lens which bends light from objects behind it

'One thing I have learned in a long life: that all our science, measured against reality, is primitive and childlike — and yet it is the most precious thing we have.'

On giants' shoulders

E INSTEIN was ever ready and careful to acknowledge the debt he owed to the scientists of the past. His generosity in this regard was a mark of the humility for which he was famous.

'[Newton's] clear and wide-ranging ideas will retain their unique significance for all time as the foundation of our whole modern conceptual structure in the sphere of natural philosophy.'

'The four men who laid the foundations of physics on which I have been able to construct my theory [of relativity] are Galileo, Newton, Maxwell and Lorentz.'

Even though the revolutionary nature of Einstein's work meant that it overturned the great theories of the past, he was adamant that it in no way invalidated what had gone before.

'The theory of relativity is nothing but another step in the centuries-old evolution of our science, one which preserves the relationships discovered in the past, deepening their insights and adding new ones.'

'Galileo was the father of modern physics – indeed, of modern science altogether.'

Galileo's universe

G ALILEO, who famously faced the Inquisition for his assertion that the Earth moves around the sun, was aware that all things are moving. Whether or not the Earth moves around the sun, even Galileo's contemporaries agreed that it spins — and so only the movement of objects relative to each other is of any consequence. This is the core of relativity, which Galileo described in 1632:

Galileo Galilei, in company with English poet John Milton

'Motion exists as motion and acts as motion in relation to things that lack it, but in regard to things that share it equally, it has no effect and behaves as if it did not exist. Thus, for example, the goods loaded on a ship move insofar as they leave Venice, go by Corfu, Crete, and Cyprus, and arrive in Aleppo, and insofar as these places (Venice, Corfu, Crete, etc.) stay still and do not move with the ship; but for the bales, boxes, and packages loaded and stowed on the ship, the motion from Venice to Syria is as nothing and in no way alters their relationship among themselves or to the ship itself; this is so because this motion is common to all and shared equally by all; on the other hand, if in this cargo a bale is displaced from a box by a mere inch, this alone is for it a greater motion (in relation to the box) than the journey of two thousand miles made by them together.'

[*Galileo Galilei*]

Physics in crisis

GALILEO'S statement of relative motion and Newton's laws of mechanics, which explain how objects move as forces operate on them, underpinned the physical sciences for two centuries.

But the old model dealt only in objects. The nineteenth century witnessed an increasing interest in phenomena such as light, sound, electricity, magnetism and radiation. These were not apparently made of matter and so confounded the traditional model of physics. In 1864, James Clerk Maxwell defined electromagnetic fields by means of four revolutionary equations.

> 'Theoretical physics have outgrown the Newtonian frame which gave stability and intellectual guidance to science for nearly two hundred years.'

To some people, it looked as though all the questions of physics had been answered. When Max Planck asked about becoming a physicist, his adviser suggested that he should try another discipline because physics was pretty much finished, with nothing else to be discovered.

But by 1884, Lord Kelvin was talking of 'clouds' on the horizon of physics which spelled trouble for the future. Inconsistencies between Newton's laws and Maxwell's equations, and between these laws and the perceived behaviour of matter, were putting theoretical physics under immense strain.

In Einstein's opinion, and in the opinion of many other scientists of the time, it was inevitable that some major breakthrough would come soon. Physics could go no further without it.

'There is no doubt that the special theory of relativity, if we look at its development in retrospect, was ripe for discovery in 1905.'

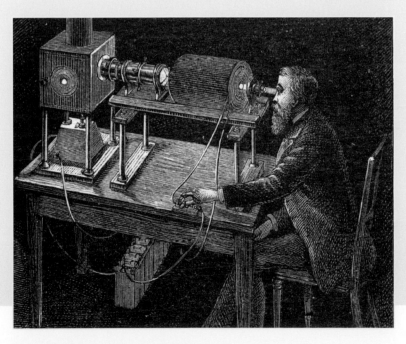

Scottish physicist James Clerk Maxwell

Light waves

THE special nature of light had long been recognized by scientists — quite how special would be revealed by Einstein. In 1678, the Dutch mathematician Christiaan Huygens suggested something similar to wave theory in order to explain the way in which light propagates.

'When one considers the extreme speed with which light spreads on every side, and how... the rays traverse one another without hindrance, one may well

Dutch mathematician and physicist Christiaan Huygens

understand that when we see a luminous object, it cannot be by any transport of matter coming to us from the object… It is in some other way that light spreads; and that which can lead us to comprehend it is the knowledge which we have of the spreading of sound in the air.'

[*Christiaan Huygens*]

Nearly 200 years later, James Clerk Maxwell used the theory of electromagnetism to explain how light and heat act as waves. As sound waves propagate through the air, light propagates as a wave.

But through what? Clerk Maxwell suggested an 'ether': a medium that was itself immobile and through which light could travel as waves. Experiments demonstrated that light did indeed act like a wave. Yet to accept the immobile ether required a rejection of relativity, which stated that nothing was completely still because everything moves relative to other objects.

'The most fascinating subject at the time that I was a student was Maxwell's theory. What made this theory appear revolutionary was the transition from forces at a distance to fields as fundamental variables.'

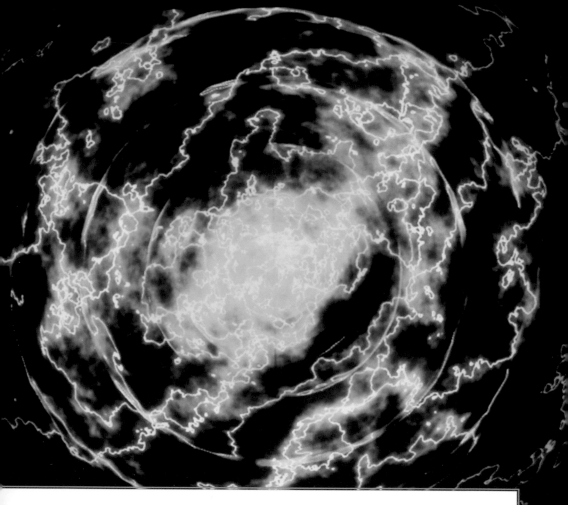

The nature of matter

THE issue of how light moved was not the only crack in the edifice of physics. There was also a problem with the very nature of matter when compared with fields, and with light in particular. Many scientists were beginning to accept that matter is made up of atoms and that the gaps between atoms are empty space.

Above: *The mapping of the electron density around a Helium atom shows the probability of an electron being in any place at a particular time, with blue the highest likelihood and red the lowest*

This makes matter discontinuous — some of it is matter and some of it is emptiness. Yet light acts like a continuous wave, with no gaps.

Light can be derived from matter — heating an electric light filament, for example, produces light, as described by Max Planck. This presented a dilemma: how could continuous light be created from discontinuous matter?

'[Before] Clerk Maxwell physical reality was conceived… as made up of material points, whose changes consist exclusively of motions… After Maxwell they conceived physical reality as represented by continuous fields, not mechanically explicable… This change in the conception of reality is the most profound and fruitful one that has come to physics since Newton; but it has at the same time to be admitted that the programme has not yet been completely carried out by any means.'

Annus mirabilis

'Nature is showing us only the tail of the lion, but I have no doubt that the lion belongs to it even though, because of its large size, it cannot totally reveal itself all at once. We can see it only the way a louse that is sitting on it would.'

In 1905, working by day in the Patent Office in Bern, Einstein published five papers which sought to untangle the problems at the heart of physics. They represented an astonishing achievement, giving the world a workable model of light, an explanation of the motion of molecules, the special theory of relativity and the basis of the famous equation $E = mc^2$.

'We have here no revolutionary act but the natural continuation of a line that can be traced through centuries.'

Einstein's third paper of 1905, *On the Electrodynamics of Moving Bodies*, introduced the special theory of relativity. It explained time, distance, mass and energy in a revolutionary way that was consistent with electromagnetism.

'The… paper is only a rough draft right now, and is an electrodynamics of moving bodies which employs a modification of the theory of space and time.'

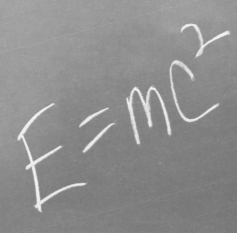

Parcels of light

'I promise you four papers in return [for Conrad Habicht sending his dissertation]. The first of which deals with radiation and the energy properties of light and is very revolutionary.'

Above: *Solar power cells convert light from the sun into usable power by means of the photoelectric effect*

Einstein's first paper, published in March 1905, built on Max Planck's work to declare that light is made of 'quanta' — little packets of energy akin to the atoms that make up matter. So both matter and light were discontinuous and subject to Newton's laws of mechanics.[1] It was this work on light that was cited for Einstein's Nobel Prize in 1921. The 'energy quanta', which we now call photons, may be absorbed by electrons which can then escape from a metallic surface — the photoelectric effect.

Light also shows wave properties, but it is not a field in motion, like the electromagnetic fields described by Clerk Maxwell, and it needs no ether through which to propagate:

'The introduction of a 'light ether' will prove superfluous.'

'When a light ray starting from a point is propagated, the energy is not continuously distributed over an ever increasing volume, but it consists of a finite number of energy quanta localised at points in space, which move without dividing and which can be absorbed or emitted only as a whole.'

[1] Newton, in fact, envisaged light in tiny packets which he called 'light corpuscles'. The idea fell out of favour when the model of light waves gained ground.

The speed of light

ONE of the postulates upon which Einstein's special theory of relativity is based is that in a universe in which everything moves, the speed of light is the only constant — light moves at the same rate irrespective of any movement of the observer. So a person running alongside a beam of light would still see it stream ahead at its fixed speed of 299,460 km per second.

'What if one were to run after a ray of light?... If one were to run fast enough, would it no longer move at all?... What is the 'velocity of light'? If it is in relation to something, this value does not hold in relation to something else which is itself in motion.'

'Light is always propagated in empty
space with a definite velocity *c* which is
independent of the state of motion of
the emitting body.'

Special relativity

I F the speed of light is the only constant, something else has to give — and that something is time. Time, in Einstein's universe, no longer moves at the same pace for everyone.

'An hour sitting with a pretty girl on a park bench passes like a minute, but a minute sitting on a hot stove seems like an hour. That is relativity.'

'My solution was really the very concept of time — that is, that time is not absolutely defined… Five weeks after my recognition of this, the present theory of special relativity was completed.'

When we lose the absolute nature of time, distance quickly follows. As a moving body approaches the speed of light, time slows down and spatial distances contract.

'Every reference-body (co-ordinate system) has its own particular time; unless we are told the reference-body to which the statement of time refers, there is no meaning in a statement of the time of an event.'

'I've completely solved the problem. My solution was to analyze the concept of time. Time cannot be absolutely defined, and there is an inseparable relation between time and signal velocity.'

Exploring simultaneity

IN Einstein's redefined universe, the time at which an event seems to take place depends on where you are standing when you watch it. Two events can seem simultaneous to one observer, but not to another.

'There is no such thing as simultaneity of distant events.'

This can be explained if we imagine two flashes of lightning, some distance apart, striking a railway embankment while a train is passing. Two people observe the flashes. One person, who is on the embankment midway between the two points, sees the flashes as simultaneous occurrences. The other person, who is on the moving train, is exactly midway between the flashes when they occur but is moving towards one and away from the other. This person sees one flash a fraction of a second before the other, since one beam of light is moving towards him or her and one is moving away — the light has different distances to travel, but its speed is the same.

Einstein contends that the flashes are both simultaneous and not simultaneous and — counter to what common sense and intuition tell us — that this is all right in the realm of physics.

Space-time

'The ordinary adult never gives a thought to space-time problems… I, on the contrary, developed so slowly that I did not begin to wonder about space and time until I was an adult. I then delved more deeply into the problem than any other adult or child would have done.'

'The non-mathematician is seized by a mysterious shuddering when he hears of 'four-dimensional' things, by a feeling not unlike that awakened by thoughts of the occult. And yet there is no more common-place statement than that the world in which we live is a four-dimensional space-time continuum.'

The possibility of treating time as a fourth dimension, comparable with the three dimensions of physical space, had been suggested before Einstein's time. Indeed, the novelist H.G. Wells had shown how a specific time could be associated with coordinates in the other three dimensions in order to locate an event uniquely in time and space, but he had not backed up the idea with the necessary mathematics. Hermann Minkowski, a professor of Einstein's who had once called him a 'lazy dog', developed Einstein's equations to give time its new status.

Hollywood's version of a time machine

Time travel

I F time slows down as the speed of travel increases, it would appear that it should be possible to travel through time. Einstein described a paradox in which a pair of twins are separated. One travels into space at a velocity close to that of light and the other remains on Earth. After fifty years (measured on Earth), the rocket returns. While the Earth-based twin has aged by fifty years, the travelling twin has aged by only ten or so years, because the speed of travel has slowed time down.

'Using faster-than-light velocities, we could telegraph into the past.'

'We conclude that a balance-wheel clock located at the Earth's equator must go more slowly, by a very small amount, than a precisely similar clock situated at one of the poles under otherwise identical conditions.'

Opposite: *In 1971, an atomic clock travelling on a very fast plane measured a slightly shorter time than an identical atomic clock left on the ground, verifying Einstein's theory that time slows at high speeds*

Of mass and energy

I T was Einstein's fourth paper of 1905 which gave the world the basis of his most famous equation and opened up the possibility of nuclear energy — and weapons. A three-page appendix to the special theory of relativity, it drew out one of the theory's most important implications:

'The theory of Clerk Maxwell and Lorentz led inevitably to the special theory of relativity... This theory made it clear that mass is not a constant quantity but depends on the energy-content – is indeed equivalent to it. It also showed that Newton's law of motion was only to be regarded as a limiting law valid for small velocities; in its place it put a new law of motion in which the speed of light in vacuo figures as the critical velocity.'

Just as time and space became inseparable under relativity, so did energy and mass.

'The inert mass of a closed system is identical with its energy, thus eliminating mass as an independent concept.'

When moving at top speed, the mass of the space shuttle is increased by about the mass of a flea because of the enormous energy involved in its motion

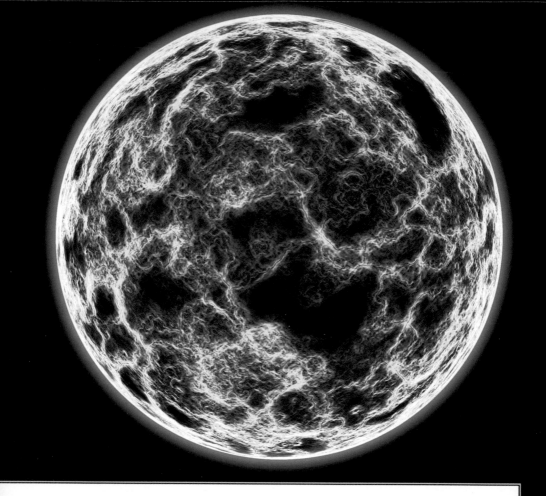

That *equation*

'We see that the term mc^2... is nothing else than the energy possessed by the body before it absorbed the energy E_0.'

Above: *The energy we get from the sun is produced by the destruction of matter. The equation reveals the energy that powers the solar system*

The equation which we now know as $E = mc^2$ was first described as $M = L/v^2$ where L is energy (later E), and v is the speed of light (later c).

'If a body releases the energy L in the form of radiation, its mass decreases by L/v^2... The mass of a body is a measure of its energy content; if the energy changes by L, the mass changes in the same sense by $L/9 \times 10^{20}$, if the energy is measured in ergs, and the mass in grams. Perhaps it will be possible to test this theory using bodies whose energy content is variable to a high degree (e.g. salts of radium).'

The relationship between mass and energy means that we can work out how much energy will be produced if we reduce the mass of a particle. As it is the mass of the particle multiplied by the square of the speed of light, and the speed of light is 299,460 km per second, it is a huge amount of energy.

The atomic age

'A consequence of the study on electrodynamics did cross my mind. The relativity principle, in association with Maxwell's fundamental equations, requires that the mass be a direct measure of the energy contained in a body; light carries mass with it. A noticeable reduction of mass would have to take place in the case of radium. The consideration is amusing and seductive; but for all I know, God Almighty might be laughing at the whole matter and might have been leading me around by the nose.'

No equipment for making such measurements existed when Einstein published his paper, and the equivalence of mass and energy was not proved until 1932 when John Cockroft and Ernest Walton used the first particle accelerator. Banesh Hoffman, who had been a student of Einstein's, commented years later:

'Imagine the audacity of such a step… Every clod of earth, every feather, every speck of dust becoming a prodigious reservoir of untapped energy. There was no way of verifying this at the time. Yet in presenting his equation in 1907 Einstein spoke of it as the most important consequence of his theory of relativity.'

Space vehicles and telecommunications satellites can use energy derived from mass through radioactive decay as a source of power

If matter could be converted entirely to energy, a single paper clip would provide the same energy as the bomb that destroyed Hiroshima. The world was a huge, untapped energy store — a nuclear power keg.

Nuclear energy

I N publishing the equation, Einstein opened a Pandora's box of nuclear energy. The conversion of mass to energy is the underlying principle of nuclear energy and nuclear weapons, both of which work by liberating energy through breaking atoms apart.

'It might be possible, and it is not even improbable, that novel sources of energy of enormous effectiveness will be opened up.'

'Concern for man himself and his fate must always constitute the chief objective of all technological endeavours... in order that the creations of our mind shall be a blessing and not a curse to mankind. Never forget this in the midst of your diagrams and equations.'

'Those who thoughtlessly make use of the miracles of science and technology, without understanding more about them than a cow eating plants understands about botany, should be ashamed of themselves.'

The atomic bomb that destroyed the Japanese city of Hiroshima contained 25 kg of uranium, about 1 kg of which was involved in the chain reaction that produced the blast. (Even this 1 kg was not converted entirely to energy — nuclear power and nuclear weapons liberate only some of the energy held in each atom.)

General relativity

THE special theory of relativity, ground-breaking as it was, represented only a beginning in Einstein's view. It was special in that it applied only in special circumstances, to bodies in constant, consistent motion. It didn't account for gravity. He wanted a theory that was generally applicable, true in all cases.

'I must observe that the theory of relativity resembles a building consisting of two separate storeys, the special theory and the general theory. The special theory, on which the general theory rests, applies to all physical phenomena with the exception of gravitation; the general theory provides the law of gravitation and its relations to the other forces of nature.'

The great physicist Max Planck warned Einstein against the endeavour:

Opposite: *Einstein in conversation with fellow physicist Max Planck*

'As an older friend, I must advise you against it for in the first place you will not succeed, and even if you succeed, no one will believe you… If you are successful, you will be the next Copernicus.'

The work was a lot harder than Einstein had envisaged and took until 1915 to complete.

'Never before in my life have I troubled myself over anything so much…
Compared with this problem, the original theory of relativity is child's play.'

'I cannot find the time to write because I am occupied with truly great things. Day and night I rack my brain in an effort to penetrate more deeply into the things that I gradually discovered in the past two years and that represent an unprecedented advance in the fundamental problems of physics.'

'In my personal experience I have hardly come to know the wretchedness of mankind better than as a result of this theory and everything connected to it.'

'Now the happy achievement seems almost a matter of course, and any intelligent student can grasp it without too much trouble. But the years of anxious searching in the dark, with their intense longing, their alterations of confidence and exhaustion and the final emergence into the light — only those who have experienced it can understand that.'

Replacing gravity

THE general theory of relativity replaces Newton's concept of gravity as a force with a completely new analogy. Instead of an attraction between objects, a distortion in the space-time continuum impels one object to move towards another.

'I was sitting in the patent office in Bern when all of a sudden a thought occurred to me: if a person falls freely, he won't feel his own weight. I was startled. This simple thought made a deep impression on me. It impelled me toward a theory of gravitation.'

Imagine a heavy person sitting on a trampoline. The trampoline dips in around the person, forming a depression. If a ball is placed on the edge of the trampoline, it will roll into the dip created by the person's weight. A planet deforms space in the same way as a heavy person deforms the trampoline, but in four dimensions — three physical dimensions and that of time. The composite of these four dimensions is space-time, or the space-time continuum, which forms the background fabric of the universe. Smaller objects deform space-time less, but still have an effect.

'When a blind beetle crawls over the surface of a curved branch, it doesn't notice that the track it has covered is indeed curved. I was lucky enough to notice what the beetle didn't notice.'

It is the deformation of space-time that controls the action of objects — and the existence of objects that defines space-time, so that without matter neither space nor time would exist. Space-time, dotted with blobs of matter ranging from vast stars to tiny specks of dust, is everywhere curved and bent by mass.

'The theory is beautiful beyond comparison. However, only one colleague has really been able to understand it.'

Curvature of space

To demonstrate the curvature of space-time and how it creates the effects of gravity, Einstein had to turn to mathematics, which he had derided and avoided for years.

'I have gained enormous respect for mathematics, whose more subtle parts I considered until now, in my ignorance, as pure luxury!'

The new theory required mastering geometry that, unlike Euclid's geometry, did not reside in planes, straight lines and points, but rolled over curved surfaces — the Gaussian geometry developed by Gauss and Riemann from 1827.

'Do not worry about your difficulties in mathematics; I can assure you that mine are still greater.'

The precession of the perihelion of Mercury had troubled astronomers since it was observed in 1859 as it seemed to refute Newton's laws. The problem was that the point at which Mercury's

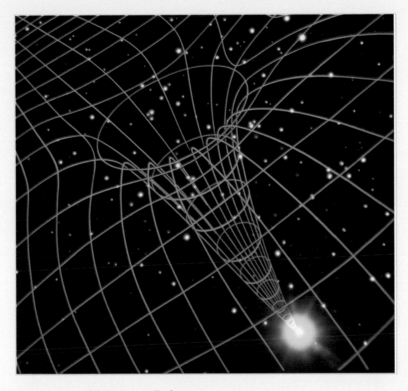

Representation of the gravity well of a star

orbit took it closest to the Sun — its perihelion — was constantly changing. It gradually moved around the Sun.

Einstein's breakthrough came when he managed to calculate the distortion in the orbit of Mercury, deriving the same result as that found by measurement. It was the moment that proved that his theory of the curvature of space was correct.

'For some days, I was beyond myself with excitement. My boldest dreams have now come true.'

Deflection of light

ACCORDING to Einstein's theory of general relativity, light would be bent by the deformation of the space-time continuum around an object such as a planet. He was proved correct by measurements taken during an eclipse in 1919 which showed, by comparing readings from different sides of the Earth, that the light from a galaxy is bent by the mass of the sun. The Astronomer Royal, Sir Frank Dyson, announced:

'After a careful study of the plates I am prepared to say that there can be no doubt that they confirm Einstein's prediction. A very definite result has been obtained that light is deflected in accordance with Einstein's law of gravitation.'

Einstein himself was not surprised. Asked how he would feel if the eclipse had not proved him correct he responded:

'I would feel sorry for the good Lord. The theory is correct anyway.'

'[Max Planck] was one of the finest people I have ever known… but he really did not understand physics… during the eclipse of 1919 he stayed up all night to see if it would confirm the bending of light by the gravitational field. If he had really understood the general theory of relativity, he would have gone to bed the way I did.'

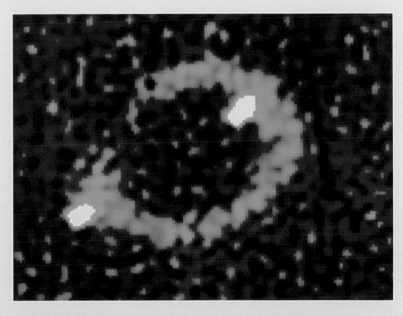

Einstein ring. The effect is produced when the light from a distant object is bent by the gravitational field of a massive body, such as a galaxy, that is situated between ourselves and the object

Redefining the universe

'When I am judging a theory, I ask myself whether, if I were God, I would have arranged the world in such a way.'

IN the space of a little over a decade, Einstein had redefined the fabric of the universe. Now, time was not a continuous stream passing relentlessly forward at the same rate, but a navigable path that could run quickly or slowly and along which we might travel in either direction. It was not counter to the space occupied by our physical universe, but part of the same fabric and could be shifted and distorted with it.

'[General relativity] takes away from space and time the last remnant of physical objectivity.'

Einstein showed the path for the physicists and cosmologists who were to come after him, setting the scene for black holes[2], Big Bang theory and the possibility of time travel.

It was not an easy ride, though. Einstein had a massive number of detractors and, amongst the more considered haranguing, he was derided for being a Jew — many German scientists wanted to rid Germany of Jewish physicists and their theories.

'Great spirits have always encountered violent opposition from mediocre minds.'

[2] Black holes were first suggested as 'dark stars' by English astronomer John Michell in 1783. He postulated a star 500 times the weight of the Sun, with such a strong gravitational field that Newton's light corpuscles could not escape from its surface.

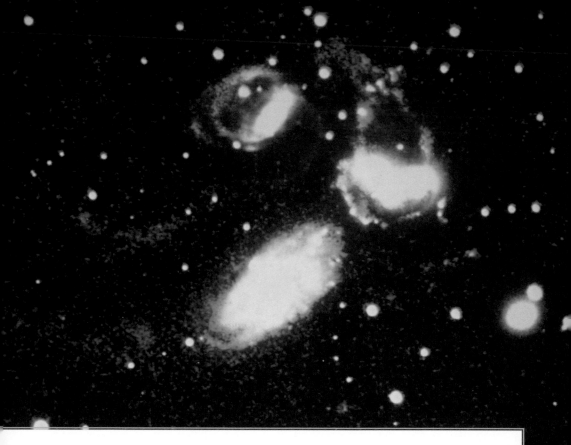

Red shifts – black holes

BLACK holes are produced when a star collapses in on itself, its gravitational field so concentrated that not even light can escape from it. At the event horizon, the boundary of the black hole's inescapable pull, light can just escape, but the photons lose energy to the dragging of gravity. This reduces the frequency of the light, pushing it towards the red end of the spectrum and creating the red shift effect. A red shift is caused by any distortion of light by gravity, but outside the arena of black holes the effect is tiny and difficult to detect.

Einstein predicted the red shift caused by the gravitational effect of the sun, but the change was so slight that he did not expect it to be measurable. It was forty years before measurements confirmed that there is indeed a gravitational red shift detectable around the sun.

'At all events, a definite decision will be reached during the next few years. If the displacement of spectral lines towards the red by the gravitational potential does not exist, then the general theory of relativity will be untenable. On the other hand, if the cause of the displacement of spectral lines be definitely traced to the gravitational potential, then the study of this displacement will furnish us with important information as to the mass of the heavenly bodies.'

Opposite: *Light from distant galaxies is shifted towards the red end of the spectrum if the galaxy is moving away from Earth, and towards the blue end of the spectrum if the galaxy is moving towards Earth. The shift is proportional to the distance from Earth and is taken as evidence of the universe's expansion*

Einstein's resistance

Aʟsᴏ at the edge of the black hole, time stands still, and space is infinitely elongated. All of these features emerge naturally from Einstein's theory of general relativity and black holes were suggested almost immediately — within a few days of Einstein's publication of the theory.

Karl Schwarzschild sent his first relativity paper to Einstein, which described his refinement of Einstein's equations and their prediction of black holes. Einstein presented it at the Prussian Academy of Sciences in Berlin in 1916. Schwarzschild developed his work further, but died a few months later, leaving black holes to lurk unexplored for the next fifty years.

Einstein found the concept of black holes, or 'Schwarzschild singularities' as they were known then, unfathomably bizarre and he resisted their existence until his death. He was not the only one to find the concept difficult. Eddington, who had led one of the teams that watched the 1919 eclipse, remarked:

'There should be a law of Nature to prevent a star behaving in this absurd way.'

Depiction of a black hole

'The essential result of this investigation is a clear understanding as to why 'Schwarzschild singularities' do not exist in physical reality.'

Black holes, however, are now almost universally accepted by astronomers.

Expanding universe

WE are now happy with the idea that the universe is expanding, but when Einstein found that the general theory of relativity suggested an expanding or contracting universe he added the 'cosmological constant' to counteract it and keep the universe stable, which he believed it was.

'[The theory] is still less satisfactory because it leads to the result that the light emitted by the stars and also individual stars of the stellar system are perpetually passing out into infinite space, never to return, and without ever again coming into interaction with other objects of nature. Such a finite material universe would be destined to become gradually but systematically impoverished.'

In 1929, Edwin Hubble showed that distant galaxies are receding — the universe really is expanding and the cosmological constant was not needed[3].

[3] Although not required by general relativity, it stays with an assumed value of zero. Occasionally, scientists suggest giving it a non-zero value. Most recently, it has been offered the role of accounting for an unknown force accelerating the expansion of the universe.

'If there is no quasi-static world, then
away with the cosmological term.'

Big Bang theory, a natural development from general relativity,
began with Georges Lemaître's suggestion in 1931 that the universe
began with an incredibly small point, a 'primeval atom', which
expanded. Einstein and Hubble both heard Lemaître lecture on his
theory of the origins of the universe.

'[Lemaître's idea] was the most beautiful
and satisfying interpretation I have ever
listened to.'

Is 'empty' space real?

C
AN empty space can be considered 'real' in any sense? The question had troubled philosophers since Descartes. The issue of whether the universe was unbounded, and whether it was expanding, gave the problem new urgency.

'Suppose that a box has been constructed. Objects can be arranged… inside the box, so that it becomes full. The possibility of such arrangements is a property of the material object 'box', something that is given with the box, the 'space enclosed' by the box… When there are no objects in the box, its space appears to be 'empty'.

'So far our concept of space has been associated with the box. It turns out, however, that the storage possibilities that make up this box-space are independent of the thickness of the walls of the box.

Cannot this thickness be reduced to zero, without the 'space' being lost as a result? The naturalness of such a limiting process is obvious, and now there remains for our thought the space without the box, a self-evident thing, yet it appears to be so unreal if we forget the origin of this concept… One can understand that it was repugnant to Descartes to consider space as independent of material objects, a thing that might exist without matter … something unsatisfactory clings to the concept of space, or to space thought of as an independent real thing.'

'… In this way, space appears as something unbounded.'

'If matter were to disappear, space and time alone would remain behind (as a kind of stage for physical happening.'

Age of the universe

'There does arise, however, a strange difficulty. The interpretation of the galactic line-shift discovered by Hubble as an expansion (which can hardly be doubted from a theoretical point of view), leads to an origin of this expansion [of the universe] which lies 'only' about 10^9 years ago, while physical astronomy makes it appear likely that the development of individual stars and systems of stars takes considerably longer. It is in no way known how this incongruity is to be overcome.'

Scientists have since re-evaluated both the age of the stars and the age of the universe, settling both at around 14 billion years. This overcomes the incongruity, supporting the general theory of relativity again.

Einstein with a group of physicists, including Erwin Hubble (2nd left)

Hubble with his telescope

Quantum mechanics

Q UANTUM mechanics, a new way of approaching and attempting to explain the behaviour of sub-atomic particles, evolved out of Einstein's description of light quanta in 1905. As such, he was the spiritual father of the movement, which emerged properly during the 1920s. It differed from the classical mechanics of Newton in fundamental respects, the most significant and worrying for Einstein being that it rested on probabilities rather than certainties.

In quantum mechanics, the position of a particle cannot be definitely given — and indeed a particle may follow an infinite number of paths at the same time. Its true position can only be stated as a probability. Einstein was never able to accept the proposition, and argued the case with all the leading physicists of his day over the last thirty years of his life.

'I don't like your kind of physics.'

Opposite: *Werner Heisenberg kick-started the quantum revolution with the exposition of his 'uncertainty principle' in 1927. Its central tenet was that 'The more precisely the position is determined, the less precisely the momentum is known in this instant, and vice versa.'*

It was not that Einstein rejected quantum mechanics entirely. He even nominated Heisenberg for the Nobel Prize three times. But he could not see it as the ultimate answer that many of his peers claimed that it was.

'This theory contains without doubt a piece of the ultimate truth.'

'I cannot but confess that I attach only a transitory importance to this interpretation.'

'The more success the quantum theory enjoys, the more stupid it looks.'

'The more one chases after quanta, the better they hide themselves.'

Of dice and atoms

'I still believe in the possibility of a model of reality — that is to say, of a theory which represents things themselves and not merely the probability of their occurrence.'

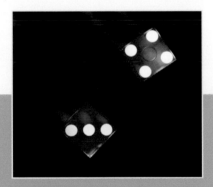

'Quantum mechanics is very worthy of regard. But an inner voice tells me that this is not yet the right track. The theory yields much, but it hardly brings us closer to the Old One's secret. I, in any case, am convinced that He does not play dice.'

Unified theory quest

FOR Einstein, the Holy Grail of physics was a single theory that would explain everything by bringing together gravitation and electromagnetism, and two forces acting at the atomic level called strong and weak forces. He hoped that such a theory would explain the behaviour of all the physical universe, from galaxies to atomic and sub-atomic particles. He called the object of his quest the unified (or unitary) field theory. Although he thought he approached it on several occasions it always eluded him.

'The purpose of my new work is to… reduce to one formula the explanation of the field of gravity and of the field of electromagnetism… Now, but only now, we know that the force which moves electrons in their ellipses about the nuclei of atoms is the same force which moves our Earth in its annual course about the sun, and is the same force which brings to us the rays of light and heat which makes life possible upon this planet.'

'At the present time, the main question is whether a field theory of the kind here contemplated can lead to the goal at all. By this is meant a theory which describes exhaustively physical reality, including four-dimensional space, by a field. The present-day generation of physicists is inclined to answer this question in the negative.... I think that... one should not desist from pursuing to the end the path of the relativistic field theory.'

As he slipped into old age, still searching for his ultimate unified theory of everything, and arguing against the latest developments in quantum theory, Einstein seemed to his contemporaries to be stuck hopelessly in the past.

'My contemporaries... see me as a heretic and a reactionary who has... outlived himself.'

'I once again sang my solitary old song.'

'I still struggle with the same problems as ten years ago. I succeed in small matters but the real goal remains unattainable, even though it sometimes seems palpably close. It is hard yet rewarding: hard because the goal is beyond my abilities, but rewarding because it makes one oblivious to the distractions of everyday life.'

'I believe that this is the God-given generalization of general relativity theory. Unfortunately, the Devil comes into play, since one cannot solve the equations [for unified field theory].'

In recent years, though, scientists have come again to look for a unified field theory — something that will be the relativity theory of the twenty-first century and heal the enduring rift between relativity and quantum mechanics.

Einstein struggled with the theory for thirty years, even asking for his notes so that he could continue to work on his deathbed, but eventually he had to admit defeat.

'Someone else is going to have to do it.'

Stephen Hawking has taken up Einstein's quest for a unified theory of everything

'The unified field theory has been put into retirement. It is so difficult to employ mathematically that I have not been able to verify it somehow, in spite of all my efforts. This state of affairs will no doubt last many more years.'

The story continues

ALTHOUGH it is for the theories of relativity that Einstein is most famous, they are not his only work. He proved the principle of Brownian motion (that molecules are constantly moving), he refined Avogadro's constant, perfecting the means of measuring the sizes of atoms and molecules, and predicted a new state of matter, called the Bose-Einstein condensate. This last was finally observed in 1995; a German and two American physicists were awarded the Nobel Prize for it in 2001.

This is not the only part of Einstein's work to bear fruit long after his death. Black holes, string theory, extra dimensions, the Big Bang and wormholes all depend on or derive from his work. Some ideas, such as wormholes (which would provide shortcuts through space-time), Einstein suggested himself, even though at the time cosmology was far behind what was needed to develop a proper model or theory.

Einstein realised, too, that gravitational fields should cause waves, moving at the speed of light, and postulated the existence of gravity waves. These were first detected in 1974 by astronomers observing a pair of neutron stars, and proved experimentally in 2005 with measurements of two orbiting pulsars.

Much more has emerged from his work which was not originally proposed by Einstein. As astronomy and cosmology have advanced, the theories of relativity have continued to have an impact, even in areas Einstein could never have dreamed of.

Heart of darkness

A hundred years on from the publication of the special theory of relativity, modern physics is in a similar dilemma to that in which Einstein found it in 1905. Before he died, Einstein recognized that a new discovery was needed to reconcile (or replace) the conflicting approaches of relativity and quantum mechanics. Both are inextricably integrated into current scientific thinking, yet they are ultimately incompatible. It seems impossible to jettison either theory, yet they can't at present be put together.

New dilemmas are testing modern physics and cosmology, and neither the theory of relativity nor quantum theory can explain them.

Since the 1960s, scientists have postulated the existence of 'dark matter' – something that we have not been able to detect, but which accounts for around 90% of the mass of the universe. Without it, galaxies should be ripped apart by the speed at which they spin. Only the possibility that they actually have more mass than we previously believed can account for their continued existence.

'Dark energy' was suggested in 1998 to explain the acceleration of the universe's expansion. Quantum theory offers the suggestion of an all-pervading 'quantum vacuum' comprising a mix of short-lived particles that wink in and out of existence, but this can't be made to work mathematically – it provides either too much or too little energy.

Together, dark energy and dark matter account for 96% of the universe – and none of our current theories can explain them. New discoveries lead to new theoretical fixes, just as they did while Newtonian physics was being stretched and patched to accommodate field theory in the late 1800s. In 1905, the patches could be discarded when Einstein re-wrote Newton. Physics today awaits a new Einstein, someone at last to find a unifying theory and fulfil his prophecy that 'someone else must do it'.

Sir Isaac Newton

RELIGION:

GOD AND RELIGION

'My position concerning God is that of an agnostic.'

Einstein was born to non-practising Jewish parents. Apart from a brief foray into religious fervour between the ages of eleven and twelve, he never observed any religion. At the age of eleven, his parents engaged a relative to teach him about the Jewish faith and for a while the young Einstein became quite fanatical in his devotions. But in the following year he discovered science and concluded that the stories he read in the Bible were just that — stories. Science became his new guide and he never again had any time for established religion, saying repeatedly that he thought it was for the naïve and fearful.

'I cannot conceive of a personal God who would directly influence the actions of individuals.'

Even so, he was not without some kind of religious sensibility.

'I am a deeply religious non-believer… This is a somewhat new kind of religion.'

Einstein attends a charity concert in the great Synagogue in the Oranienburgerstreet in Berlin

Despite denying the existence of a 'personal' God, Einstein spoke frequently of God. So frequently, in fact, that Friedrich Dürrenmatt commented: 'I was led to suspect he was a closet theologian'. But what Einstein meant by God was not the Judaeo-Christian God who spoke to humankind through prophets and laws. Instead he saw the hand of a great and unknowable intelligence at work in the laws of physics.

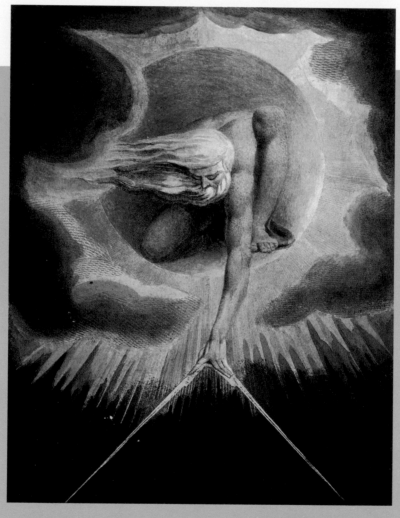

The Ancient of Days, William Blake's stunning vision of God as the designer of the universe

'I'm not an atheist and I don't think I can
call myself a pantheist. We are in the
position of a little child entering a huge
library filled with books in many different
languages. The child knows someone
must have written those books. It does
not know how. It does not understand the
languages in which they are written. The
child dimly suspects a mysterious order in
the arrangement of the books but doesn't
know what it is. That, it seems to me, is
the attitude of even the most intelligent
human being toward God. We see a
universe marvelously arranged and
obeying certain laws, but only dimly
understand these laws. Our limited minds
cannot grasp the mysterious force that
moves the constellations.'

Denying a frail god

E INSTEIN could not accept the idea of a deity that might take any interest in the affairs of human beings.

'The idea of a personal God is quite alien to me and seems even naïve.'

'I cannot imagine a God who rewards and punishes the objects of his creation, whose purposes are modeled after our own — a God, in short, who is but a reflection of human frailty.'

Whether or not Einstein believed in God became something of a celebrated question as he became more famous. A New York rabbi once asked him by telegram:

'Do you believe in God? Stop. Prepaid reply fifty words.'

Einstein replied (with words to spare):

'I believe in Spinoza's God who reveals himself in the orderly harmony of what exists, not in a God who concerns himself with the fate and actions of human beings.'

For Einstein, a personal God was diminishing for humankind, whose right behaviour then becomes a matter of purely personal gain.

'Man would indeed be in a poor way if he had to be restrained by fear of punishment and hope of reward after death.'

The gates of Auschwitz

In Einstein's view moral behaviour, or concern for others, was an obligation born of our humanity, not something that should be related to religion.

'Morality is of the highest importance — but for us, not God.'

Like many people before and since, Einstein found the world too hostile a place for him to be able to sustain a belief in a God that could intervene to alleviate suffering, but does not do so.

'I see only with deep regret that God punishes so many of his children for their numerous stupidities, for which he himself can be held responsible; in my opinion, only his non-existence could excuse him.'

Body and soul

NEITHER could Einstein believe in a separation of the body and soul, a division which had seemed self-evident to philosophers from antiquity until the 17th century. In part, this was because he refused to believe in a portion of the human being that could survive death. He felt this belief to be a cowardly way of dealing with mortality, and a demonstration of the arrogance that could not accept the short duration of an individual's period of influence in the universe.

'I do not believe in immortality of the individual.'

'I cannot conceive… nor would I want to conceive of an individual who survives his physical death; let feeble souls, from fear or absurd egoism, cherish such thoughts.'

But there was more to his refusal of a separate soul than humility in the face of an infinite universe. He could see no space for anything that might be a soul suffusing a physical entity. If matter is interchangeable with energy anyway, what and where would the 'soul' be?

'The concept of a soul without a body seems to me to be empty and devoid of meaning.'

'I am fascinated by Spinoza's pantheism, but admire even more his contributions to modern thought because he is the first philosopher to deal with the soul and body as one, not two separate things.'

Spinoza and pantheism

EINSTEIN was greatly impressed by the work of the Dutch Jew, Benedict de Spinoza (1632–77). As a Rationalist, Spinoza denied that our senses play a particularly important part in the acquisition of knowledge, preferring to put his faith in pure reason. He advanced geometry as a model for philosophy, a position which was bound to appeal to Einstein.

Einstein was drawn to Spinoza's philosophy because of three principal points on which Spinoza departed from Descartes and previous philosophers. Spinoza rejected the claims that we can examine a relationship between man and God, that we can meaningfully speak separately of the body and soul, and that we can account for actions according to freewill exhibited by God and man.

In his *Ethics*, Spinoza spelt out his pantheistic religion, developing the impossibility of a relationship between man and God. The Christians and Jews who were his contemporaries saw nature as the finest work of God, but Spinoza saw it as God itself. For him, God was in all things and was the system of physical and natural laws which governs the universe. Einstein's position differed slightly in that he did not see nature as God, but as the perfect and inevitable embodiment of the rules governing the universe, which could be discovered at least partially through reason.

'I will call it the cosmic religious sense. This is hard to make clear to those who do not experience it, since it does not involve an anthropomorphic idea of God; the individual feels the vanity of human desires and aims, and the nobility and marvellous order which are revealed in nature and in the world of thought.'

Einstein did not seek a purpose or meaning in the universe, but only a beautifully ordered structure which we can imperfectly understand.

The mind of God

THE workings of the universe inspired an awe in Einstein that he sometimes termed 'religious'. At least once he called this sense 'pantheistic', after Spinoza, but more often he used his own term, 'cosmic religion'.

'[The scientist's] religious feeling takes the form of a rapturous amazement at the harmony of natural law, which reveals an intelligence of such superiority that, compared with it, all the systematic thinking and acting of human beings is utterly insignificant reflection.'

His reference to an intelligence behind the structure of the universe or the laws of nature does not require a god in the usual sense of the word, a being who takes an interest in or even recognizes or acknowledges the existence of humanity.

'The beginnings of cosmic religious feeling already appear at an early stage of development, e.g., in many of the Psalms of David and in some of the Prophets. Buddhism... contains a much stronger element of this.'

Benedict de Spinoza's pantheism appealed greatly to Einstein

'It is precisely among the heretics of every age that we find men who were filled with this highest kind of religious feeling and were in many cases regarded by their contemporaries as atheists.'

With or without man

As a scientist, Einstein accepted *a priori* the existence of the external universe.

'The belief in an external world independent of the perceiving subject is the basis of all natural science.'

The question then arises of how central human consciousness is to the existence of everything that is not physical matter. With the Hindu poet Rabindranath Tagore, Einstein discussed the existence of abstract concepts, truth and beauty, outside the realm of the human mind. On beauty they agreed that it is a construct of human perception. On truth, they disagreed. For Tagore, truth was 'one with the Universal Being' and as such must be essentially human. Religious believers, whether Jew, Christian, Muslim or Hindu, posit a being which is greater than human but of which the human is some kind of image or shadowing, however fragmentary or imperfect. As this being 'is' truth, truth is essentially human as Tagore argued.

For Einstein, this link with the human in truth was completely redundant. His firm belief that truth is completely independent of human consciousness set him apart from most religious and scientific thinkers.

'I cannot prove that scientific truth must be conceived as a truth that is valid independent of humanity; but I believe it firmly. I believe, for instance, that the Pythagorean theorem of geometry states something that is approximately true, independent of the existence of man. Anyway, if there is a reality independent of man, there is also a truth relative to this reality; and in the same way the negation of the first engenders a negation of the existence of the latter.'

Einstein coined the term 'objective reality' for independent existence of truth, outside the human mind.

A religion for scientists

THIS awareness of an unknowable, designing intelligence behind the universe became a kind of religion for Einstein and for many physicists of the age. But it shared no part of the mythology of established religions.

'I see a pattern, but my imagination cannot picture the maker of that pattern. I see a clock, but I cannot envision the clockmaker. The human mind is unable to conceive of the four dimensions, so how can it conceive of a God, before whom a thousand years and a thousand dimensions are as one?'

The intelligent design that Einstein saw in the universe bore no resemblance at all to that proposed by Christian fundamentalists who oppose the teaching of evolution. The designer imagined by Einstein did not plan or intend the existence of any beings, but created only the laws from which all else inevitably followed.

'My religiosity consists of a humble admiration of the infinitely superior spirit that reveals itself in the little that we can comprehend of the knowable world. That deeply emotional conviction of the presence of a superior reasoning power, which is revealed in the incomprehensible universe, forms my idea of God.'

'How can cosmic religious feeling be communicated from one person to another, if it can give rise to no definite notion of a God and no theology? In my view, it is the most important function of art and science to awaken this feeling and keep it alive in those who are receptive to it.'

Science, religion, art

EINSTEIN did not see religion and science in opposition to one another, but saw both inspired by the same feeling, one for which he had immense admiration.

'The most beautiful and deepest experience a man can have is the sense of the mysterious. It is the underlying principle of religion as well as of all serious endeavor in art and science.'

Science is perhaps in tension with established religion in that it endeavours to uncover knowledge and does not accept that anything should, of necessity, be unknowable — even if some things might be too difficult to discover. Einstein did not have any expectation of revelation. As his view of the universe was not anthropocentric, he expected nature to be inexplicable and was surprised that mankind could uncover any of nature's laws.

'If God created the world, his primary concern was certainly not to make its understanding easy for us.'

'The scientist has to worm these principles out of nature.'

In his search for a unified field theory, Einstein realized that he was trying to uncover the secrets at the heart of the universe, the divine master plan, if there was one. Here religion and science come together.

'I want to know how God created the world. I am not interested in this or that phenomenon, in the spectrum of this or that element. I want to know His thoughts, the rest are details.'

Lessons from the past

EINSTEIN was keen not to throw the baby of morality out with the bath water of established religion, however. He remained deeply impressed by the moral teachings of some of the great religious figures of world history, even though he rejected their divinity. He greatly valued the impetus to moral living provided by religious teaching, which he considered the principal value of religion.

'What humanity owes to personalities like Buddha, Moses, and Jesus ranks for me higher than all the achievements of the enquiring and constructive mind...'

'More and more I come to value charity and love of one's fellow being above everything else... All our lauded technological progress — our very civilization — is like the axe in the hand of the pathological criminal.'

Yet he also saw that most religious people did not follow the more useful teachings of religion, so the benefit was largely lost.

'If the believers of the present-day religions would earnestly try to think and act in the spirit of the founders of these religions then no hostility on the basis of religion would exist among the followers of the different faiths. Even the conflicts in the realm of religion would be exposed as insignificant.'

Better than nothing

E INSTEIN felt that a belief in a personal God, a God who
intervened in the doings of humankind was, for most people,
the only way to achieve a moral and transcendental outlook on life
and so was preferable to outright atheism.

'Such a belief [in a personal God] seems
to me preferable to the lack of any
transcendental outlook on life, and I
wonder whether one can ever
successfully render to the majority of
mankind a more sublime means in order
to satisfy its metaphysical needs.'

Einstein certainly did not think religious feeling was redundant. He
felt that while science shows us what *is*, religion must show us what
we should do, helping us to set the goals of human aspirations.

'To make clear these fundamental ends and valuations, and to set them fast in the emotional life of the individual, seems to me precisely the most important function which religion has to perform in the social life of man.'

The Grand Orrery, a mechanical model of the solar system

A determinist universe

'Everything is determined, the beginning as well as the end, by forces over which we have no control. It is determined for the insect as well as for the star. Human beings, vegetables, or cosmic dust, we all dance to a mysterious tune, intoned in the distance by an invisible player.'

Einstein's model of the physical universe, in which all that happens is governed by immutable laws, left no role for an interventionist God.

The question of free will: Einstein believed it to be a necessary illusion

'The man who is thoroughly convinced of the universal operation of the law of causation cannot for a moment entertain the idea of a being who interferes in the course of events... a man's actions are determined by necessity, external and internal, so that in God's eyes he cannot be responsible, any more than an inanimate object is responsible for the motions it undergoes.'

It left no space for human free will; the question remained whether Einstein's determinist universe left any space for God to exercise free will.

'I am a determinist, compelled to act as if free will existed, because if I wish to live in a civilized society, I must act responsibly.'

'What really interests me is whether God could have created the world any differently; in other words, whether the demand for logical simplicity leaves any freedom at all.'

WAR:

EINSTEIN'S
PACIFISM

'I am opposed to the use of force under
any circumstances except when
confronted by an enemy who pursues the
destruction of life as an end in itself.'

Einstein was always strongly opposed to war, which he referred to
as 'that savage and unworthy relic of the age of barbarism.'
He was one of the few scientists who refused to sign a petition
supporting German nationalism in the move towards war in 1914.
It was a position that he maintained all his life, despite his regretful
support for the war against Nazi Germany.

'That worst outcrop of herd life, the military system, which I abhor…ought to be abolished with all possible speed.'

'How vile and despicable war seems to me! I would rather be hacked into pieces than take part in such an abominable business.'

'To my mind, to kill in war is not a whit better than to commit ordinary murder.'

German troops on the march, 1914

The military mindset

FROM the time of his own youth, when he had moved out of Germany to avoid compulsory military service, Einstein had always been an enemy of conscription. He found it abominable that a state could force its citizens to do something that they disapproved of, and even deride or punish them for their strong moral fibre if they refused. The state was overstepping the limits of its authority over individuals, he felt, when it compelled people to undertake military service. It was also fostering the kind of nationalism and patriotism that leads to conflict, as it had in the First World War.

'The state should be our servant and not we its slaves. The state transgresses this commandment when it compels us by force to engage in military and war service, the more so since the object and effect of this slavish service is to kill people belonging to other countries or interfere with their freedom of development.'

'The greatest obstacle to international order is that monstrously exaggerated spirit of nationalism which also goes by the fair-sounding but misused name of patriotism.'

German First World War leaders Paul Hindenburg, Kaiser Wilhelm, Erich Ludendorff

'Compulsory military service, as the hotbed of unhealthy nationalism, must be combated; most important of all, conscientious objectors must be protected on an international basis.'

A stand against war

ONSCIENTIOUS objectors were universally reviled during the First World War. Einstein stood against the tide by expressing his huge respect and admiration for those who refused to fight.

'Is the severe persecution to which conscientious objectors to military service are subjected today a whit less disgraceful to the community than those

Above: 'The Menin Road 1919' by war artist Paul Nash

to which the martyrs of religion were exposed in former centuries?'

'More dreadful even than the destruction [of war], in my opinion, is the humiliating slavery into which war plunges the individual. Is it not a terrible thing to be forced by society to do things which all of us as individuals regard as abominable crimes? Only a few had the moral greatness to resist; them I regard as the real heroes of the World War.'

Much later in his life, he campaigned with Bertrand Russell and others against war. And after the atomic bombs dropped on Japan in 1945 he came up with a special class of conscientious objector, the non-participating scientist.

'Noncooperation in military matters should be an essential moral principle for all true scientists ... who are engaged in basic research.'

Einstein and the bomb

'As long as there is man, there will be war.'

Einstein's humanism, coupled with his lack of belief in a personal God, led directly to his powerful feeling that humankind holds its fate in its own hands. For Einstein, it became perfectly possible to imagine that humankind could wreak terrible devastation with nuclear weapons — there was no benign, overseeing God to protect His creation.

27 Mar 1954, Bikini Atoll, Marshall Islands. The 11 megaton bomb 'Romeo' is tested during Operation Castle

Einstein was a confirmed pacificist long before the advent of nuclear weapons brought a new and terrible threat to the world. He had avoided military service in Germany as a very young man by moving out of the country and throughout his life he deplored conscription and military education.

When Einstein recognized the huge reserves of power hidden in every atom he found the key to atomic power and atomic weapons. He did not, at first, think it likely that he would ever see that energy unleashed in his lifetime and so he was not alarmed at the distant prospect of nuclear war. He thought that harnessing the power of the atom would be as difficult

'as firing at birds in the dark, in a neighborhood that has few birds.'

Ernest Rutherford, whose work led to the discovery of the nucleus of the atom, did not consider atomic bombs a realistic proposition either, saying

'Anyone who expects a source of power from the transformation of these atoms is talking moonshine.'

The bomb a reality

However, Einstein had always been aware that the energy locked within the atom might one day be released — and that it could be used for evil purposes as well as for good.

He had no illusions about the dire consequences that might follow once that power was released.

'Assuming that it were possible to effect that immense energy release, we should merely find ourselves in an age compared to which our coal-black present would seem golden.'

'All bombardments since the invention of firearms put together would be harmless child's play compared to its destructive effects.'

The atomic bomb became a much more realizable prospect with the discovery of the neutron by James Chadwick in 1932. And in 1939, when Enrico Fermi and Leo Szilard succeeded in releasing two neutrons from the nucleus of a uranium atom, the race for an atomic chain reaction was on. If the two released neutrons could be used to split another two atoms, releasing a total of four more neutrons, and these were used to split a further four atoms, releasing eight neutrons, and so on, the bomb could perhaps be made. Even so, Fermi himself thought at the start that there was:

'little likelihood of an atomic bomb, little proof that we were not pursuing a chimera.'

The Westinghouse 'atom smasher' in which particles are accelerated to 100,000,000 mph

The Nazi threat

WHEN Enrico Fermi demonstrated the nuclear chain reaction that made atomic weapons a reality, Einstein was horrified at the possibilities it opened up. Even though he had been a confirmed pacifist all his life, he still encouraged the development of atomic weapons in the Second World War. This may seem a curious *volte-face*, yet he did so only because he feared that the Nazis would develop a nuclear weapon first, with dire consequences for the world.

'We helped in creating this new weapon in order to prevent the enemies of mankind from achieving it ahead of us, which, given the mentality of the Nazis, would have meant inconceivable destruction and the enslavement of the rest of the world.'

Einstein recognized that the brutality and ruthlessness of the Nazis constituted a special case. Refusing to rise against them was not a viable option, he realized, though other pacificists still hoped for a solution without all-out war.

'The anti-militarists are falling on me as on a wicked renegade… those fellows simply wear blinders.'

'It is unworthy of a great nation to stand idly by while small countries of great culture are being destroyed with a cynical contempt for justice.'

'Organized power can be opposed only by organized power. Much as I regret this, there is no other way.'

Massed ranks of Nazi Party members at the 1934 Nuremberg rally

Building the bomb

'Had I known that the Germans would not succeed in producing an atomic bomb, I never would have lifted a finger.'

In 1939, at the prompting of Fermi and Szilard, Einstein signed a letter to President Roosevelt which outlined the possibilities of nuclear weapons derived from uranium. It also highlighted the actions of the Nazis who, in Czechoslovakia, were sealing off mines that were a rich source of uranium ore. The letter encouraged research that might lead to the creation of a nuclear weapon ahead of the Nazis. Einstein would later say that signing the letter was his greatest mistake.

Along with later reports to Washington, Einstein's letter led to the Manhattan Engineering Project: it was set up secretly in 1941, under the direction of J. Robert Oppenheimer, with the aim of developing a nuclear weapon.

'I have done no work on [the atomic bomb], no work at all. I am interested in the bomb the same as any other person, perhaps a little bit more interested.'

Einstein himself was not asked to participate in the development, though he noticed that many of his colleagues disappeared to work in New Mexico. The US government did not consider him sufficiently trustworthy to be included in so secret and critical a development. The FBI concluded:

'In view of his radical background, this office would not recommend the employment of Dr Einstein, on matters of a secret nature, without a very careful investigation, as it seems unlikely that a man of his background could, in such a short time, become a loyal American citizen.'

I understand that Germany has actually stopped the sale of uranium from the Czechoslovakian mines which she has taken over. That she should have taken such early action might perhaps be understood on the ground that the son of the German Under-Secretary of State, von Weizsäcker, is attached to the Kaiser-Wilhelm-Institut in Berlin where some of the American work on uranium is now being repeated.

Yours very truly,

A. Einstein

(Albert Einstein)

Extract from Einstein's letter to President Theodore Roosevelt, 2 August 1939, in which he raises the possibility that Germany could develop an atomic bomb

Armageddon realized

THE bomb, finally developed in 1945, was dropped on Japan three months after the defeat of the Nazis. There had been no suggestion that the Japanese might develop atomic weapons. On hearing the news, Einstein said only

'Oh, Weh.'

Pressed for an opinion, he remained silent, instructing his personal secretary Helen Dukas to release this statement:

'Military expediency demands that he remain uncommunicative on the subject until the authorities release details.'

He reserved public comment on whether the bomb should have been dropped for a year, then in 1946 The New York Times carried an article in which he made his views known:

'Prof. Albert Einstein… said that he was sure that President Roosevelt would have forbidden the atomic bombing of

Hiroshima had he been alive and that it was probably carried out to end the Pacific war before Russia could participate.'

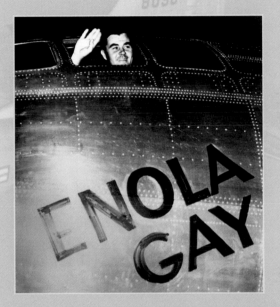

The Enola Gay, the B-29 bomber used to drop the atomic bomb on Hiroshima

'I have always condemned the use of the atomic bomb against Japan.'

After the war, Einstein returned to his former position of pacificism, campaigning relentlessly for peace and for the non-proliferation of nuclear weapons. He believed that only an international peace-keeping force, replacing national armies, and a world government could offer any chance of sustained peace.

Mistakes and regrets

By discovering the source of the power that was eventually unleashed in nuclear weapons, Einstein has been implicated in, and sometimes even blamed for, the arrival of the nuclear age. It is as though it were a crime that he personally perpetrated against humanity.

Although he frequently wrote of the regret and even guilt that scientists felt about the ways in which atomic energy was used, he refused to take responsibility for something which is, finally, a law of physics.

'I do not consider myself the father of the release of atomic energy. My part in it was quite indirect. I did not, in fact, foresee that it would be released in my time. I believed only that it was theoretically possible.'

'I made one great mistake in my life — when I signed the letter to President

Roosevelt recommending that atom bombs be made; but there was some justification — the danger that the Germans would make them.'

'I was fully aware of the terrible danger to mankind in case this attempt [to produce an atomic bomb] succeeded. But the likelihood that the Germans were working on the same problem with a chance of succeeding forced to me this step [of signing the letter to Roosevelt]. I could do nothing else although I have always been a convinced pacifist.'

Einstein on the cover of Time *magazine, 1 July, 1946*

'It is strange that science, which in the old days seemed harmless, should have evolved into a nightmare that causes everyone to tremble.'

After the war

E INSTEIN was not impressed by the performance of the USA and the UK in the wake of the war.

'We delivered this weapon into the hands of the American and the British people as trustees of the whole of mankind, as fighters for peace and liberty. But so far

Devastation at Hiroshima, preserved as a memorial to the dead

we fail to see any guarantee of peace, we
do not see any guarantee of the freedoms
that were promised to the nations… The
world was promised freedom from fear,
but in fact fear has increased
tremendously since the termination of
the war. The world was promised
freedom from want, but large parts of the
world are faced with starvation while
others are living in abundance. The
nations were promised liberation and
justice. But we have witnessed, and are
witnessing even now, the sad spectacle of
'liberating' armies firing into populations
who want their independence and social
equality, and supporting in those
countries, by force of arms, such parties
and personalities as appear to be most
suited to serve vested interests.'

'The war is won, but the peace is not.'

Einstein spent the rest of his life campaigning for the control of nuclear weapons and the formation of a world government to help control the use of arms.

'Striving for peace and preparing for war are incompatible with each other ... Arms must be entrusted only to an international authority.'

'People are living now just as they were before [the war]... and it is clear that they have learned nothing from the horrors which they have had to deal with.'

He despaired that in the 1950s the USA was again stockpiling weapons and was exhibiting crippling paranoia about the supposed threat of communism.

'The real ailment [is]... the belief that we must in peacetime so organize our life and work that in the event of war we would be sure of victory... This attitude

Soviet military parade during the Cold War era

… must, if it does not rectify itself, lead to war and to very far-reaching destruction.'

For Einstein, only the total renunciation of war offered any hope for the future.

'War is not a parlor game in which the players obediently stick to the rules. Where life and death are at stake, rules and obligations go by the board. Only the absolute repudiation of all war can be of any use here.'

Against destruction

'The discovery of nuclear chain reactions need not bring about the destruction of mankind, any more than did the discovery of matches. We only must do everything in our power to safeguard against its abuse.'

To safeguard the world, though, Einstein knew that it would take responsible government and a complete change in the traditions of nationalism and patriotism to keep the threat posed by the bomb at bay.

US soldiers in Vietnam, where the USA and the USSR fought one another by proxy

'The physicists who participated in forging the most formidable and dangerous weapon of all times are harassed by [a]… feeling of responsibility, not to say guilt. We cannot and should not slacken in our efforts to make the nations of the world, and especially their governments, aware of the unspeakable disaster they are certain to provoke unless they change their attitude toward each other.'

He saw, too, that cultural tolerance must be a cornerstone of future peace — a warning that the early 21st century has yet to heed.

'A world federation [the United Nations] presupposes a new kind of loyalty on the part of man, a sense of responsibility that does not stop short at the national boundaries. Understanding among different cultural groups, mutual economic and cultural aid are the necessary additions.'

World government

EINSTEIN concluded that national armies could never be compatible with world peace. Instead, he felt, a global military force that could be deployed against rogue nations seeking to oppress or invade others could offer the only guarantee of peace. This necessarily involved surrendering some of the powers and autonomy that individual nations enjoyed — but he felt that to do otherwise would come at too high a cost.

'Anybody who really wants to abolish war must resolutely declare himself in favour of his own country's resigning a portion of its sovereignty in favour of international institutions: he must be ready to make his own country amenable, in case of a dispute, to the award of an international court. He must, in the most uncompromising fashion, support disarmament all round.'

'We must not be merely willing,
but actively eager, to submit ourselves
to the binding authority necessary for
world security.'

*UN building, New York. UN forces have often proven less effective than
Einstein hoped*

'Any government is certain to be evil to
some extent. But a world government is
preferable to the far greater evil of wars.'

'The only salvation for civilisation…
lies in the creation of a world government,
with security of nations founded upon
law… As long as sovereign states continue
to have separate armaments and armaments
secrets, new world wars will be inevitable.'

The atomic future

EINSTEIN was certain of the dangers of continuing with the arms race once nuclear weapons were in the armoury. But he sometimes despaired of mankind making the necessary changes.

'Through the release of atomic energy, our generation has brought into the world the most revolutionary force since prehistoric man's discovery of fire.'

'I do not know how the Third World War will be fought, but I can tell you what they will use in the Fourth — rocks!'

'The unleashing of power of the atom bomb has changed everything except our mode of thinking, and thus we head toward unparalleled catastrophes.'

Philosopher and peace campaigner Bertrand Russell

Einstein's last signed statement before he died was issued jointly with English philosopher Bertrand Russell in April 1955:

'There lies before us, if we choose, continued progress in happiness, knowledge, and wisdom. Shall we, instead, choose death, because we cannot forget our quarrels? We appeal, as human beings, to human beings: Remember your humanity and forget the rest.'

POLITICS:
A RELUCTANT POLITICIAN

'Politics are for the moment.
An equation is for eternity.'

Einstein was an unlikely politician. He was a man who enjoyed solitude, doing his best work when left to think on his own, a scientist whose intellectual work was so complex that few people could understand it and a refugee who claimed to have no home state. So he was not the sort of person we might expect to find acting in the political arena.

His involvement in politics was a response to his status as a Jew during a time of persecution and his conviction as a pacifist. These factors contributed to his alienation from Germany and led him to speak out, and to put forward views that were under-represented. But it was his fame as a physicist and his popularity as a humanist that made people listen to what he said.

He was under no illusion that it was often his name, rather than his wisdom, that was wanted by the cause.

'I am needed not for my abilities but solely for my name, from whose publicity value a substantial effect is expected among the rich tribal companions in Dollaria [the USA].'

Because he was famous and popular, he could command the attention of influential people — hence Roosevelt read and acted on his letter about the atomic bomb.

'What better use could a person make of his 'name' than to speak out publicly from time to time if he believes it necessary?'

Prime Minister Jawaharlal Nehru of India meets Einstein at Einstein's home

Zionism vs. Judaism

EINSTEIN'S phase as a religious Jew was a passing childhood enthusiasm. In line with his views on religion generally he later had little sympathy for practising Jews, whom he thought 'naïve'. He described a visit to the Wailing Wall in Jerusalem:

'Where dull-witted clansmen of our tribe were praying aloud, their faces turned to the wall, their bodies swaying to and fro. A pathetic sight of men with a past but without a future.'

Above: *The Wailing Wall in Jerusalem*

That Einstein himself was not Jewish by religion made no difference to those in Europe who were rising up against the Jews, and he soon found Jewish identity forced upon him. He grew to see it as his own and felt that it was not dependent on, or even necessarily related to, the Jewish religion.

'What characterizes a Jew is not his faith but his membership in the Jewish nationality.'

'When I read of 'German citizens of the Jewish faith,' I cannot avoid a wry smile. What is concealed behind that pretty name? What is Jewish faith? Is there a kind of non-faith through which one ceases to be a Jew? No… To speak of faith is a way of hiding that what characterizes a Jew is not his faith but his membership in the Jewish nationality. We must learn again to take pride in our history, and as a people we must resume the cultural tasks that can renew our community feeling.'

The Jewish tribesman

'I am by heritage a Jew, by citizenship Swiss, and by makeup a human being, and *only* a human being, without any special attachment to any state or national entity whatsoever.'

Einstein developed a strong sense of identity with other Jews. There was no country that he could regard as home so his Jewish identity was the only sense he had of being part of a community or tribe. He was increasingly sympathetic towards the plight of Jews and the Zionist cause. In this he was spurred on by the abuse of the Jewish people in Nazi Germany and the failure of the rest of Europe to raise a finger to help them.

'My relationship to the Jewish people has become my strongest human bond, ever since I became fully aware of our precarious situation among the nations of the world.'

He fought against the persecution of Jews, and helped Jews displaced by the Nazis to settle in America. He became politically involved in the founding of Israel and he promoted peace with Palestine and the foundation of a Jewish University. (The Hebrew University in Jerusalem now houses the 40,000 documents of his archive.) In return, he was offered the presidency of Israel. He wisely turned it down.

'I should much rather see a reasonable agreement with the Arabs based on living together in peace than the creation of a Jewish state.'

On democracy

'The only justifiable purpose of political institutions is to assure the unhindered development of the individual.'

Einstein receives a cheque from Henry Morgenthau Sr. for the children of German Jewish refugees

Einstein believed strongly that each individual has a responsibility to work for what he or she thinks right and that it is necessary to stand up against injustice and speak out, however unpopular or difficult it might prove. It was a creed he lived by all his life. With no personal God to step in and save any individual, or humankind in general, personal responsibility and action were paramount.

'In these days of democratic government the fate of nations hangs on the people themselves; each individual must always bear that in mind.'

'The individual must not merely wait and criticize. He must serve the cause as best he can. The fate of the world will be such as the world deserves.'

Personal responsibility and morality were for Einstein inextricable. Morality was not an issue of religion, but of personal dignity and a life worth living.

'The fate of the human race [is] more than ever dependent on its moral strength today. The way to a joyful and happy existence is everywhere through renunciation and self-limitation.'

'Only morality in our actions can give beauty and dignity to life.'

US witch-hunts

THE US government was suspicious of Einstein. His outspokenness and his unwillingness to toe any party line led to his exclusion from the Manhattan Project, which was formed to develop nuclear weapons (though he was no doubt glad to have had no part in it). Later, he denounced the anti-Communist witch-hunts of the McCarthy years and the investigations of the House Un-American Activities Committee.

'I have never been a Communist. But if I were, I would not be ashamed of it.'

'The fear of communism has led to practices that have become incomprehensible to the rest of civilized mankind and expose our country to ridicule.'

'Refusal to testify must be based on the assertion that it is shameful for a blameless citizen to submit to such an inquisition and that this kind of inquisition violates the spirit of the Constitution.'

Einstein with son and grandson

'I hardly ever felt as alienated from people as I do right now… The worst is that nowhere is there anything with which one can identify. Brutality and lies are everywhere.'

The role of the state

E INSTEIN renounced Germany early on to avoid military service, lived in Switzerland and Italy, and rejected his homeland once again on the rise of the Nazis. When visiting Winston Churchill in England he wrote 'None' under 'Address' in

Above: Einstein's original Swiss passport; he would later declare himself stateless

the visitors' book. The only sense of belonging that he ever laid claim to was as part of the Jewish 'tribe'. Perhaps this statelessness gave him a particular vantage point for pondering the relationship between state and individual.

'Nationalism is an infantile disease. It is the measles of mankind.'

'When the state becomes the main thing and the individual becomes its weak-willed tool, then all finer values are lost. Just as the rock must first crumble for trees to grow on it, and just as the soil must first be loosened for its fruitfulness to develop, so too can valuable achievement sprout from human society only when it is sufficiently loosened so as to make possible to the individual the free development of his activities.'

PHILOSOPHY:
THE UNIVERSE
AT LARGE

'What Einstein said wasn't all that stupid.'

[*Wolfgang Pauli*]

Einstein thought, wrote and spoke about a broad range of subjects. He was often approached for comments or articles and he corresponded at length with some of the greatest figures of his day including Niels Bohr, Erwin Schrödinger, Marie Curie, Paul Ehrenfest, Hendrik Lorentz, Mahatma Gandhi, President Theodore Roosevelt, Winston Churchill and Chaim Weizmann. He debated not just with scientists and politicians but with great intellectuals in other fields such as Sigmund Freud, Bertrand Russell, Bertolt Brecht and Rabindranath Tagore.

After his emigration to the USA, he came to be regarded as an all-purpose genius, something of an oracle, whose pronouncements on almost any topic carried weight. Members of the public from around the world wrote to him with praise, criticism, random abuse and even offers of marriage. He was so famous that letters addressed to 'Dr Einstein, USA' were delivered correctly — a distinction he probably shares only with heads of state and Father Christmas.

Einstein with fellow physicist and Nobel Prize winner Marie Curie, 1925

As well as writing on weighty and universal matters, he reflected sometimes on his life — and later on his mortality and approaching death. Though he had no expectation of an afterlife, he viewed death with equanimity and without fear, dignified to the end.

On knowledge

'One enigma has continued to trouble research scientists since time immemorial. How is it possible that mathematics, which after all is a product of human thought independent of experience, applies so perfectly to real objects? Can human reason discover the properties of real things by thought alone, without the help of experience?... It seems to me that... insofar as mathematical propositions refer to reality, they are not certain, and insofar as they are certain, they do not refer to reality.'

'In a certain sense, then, I hold it true that pure thought can grasp reality, as the ancients dreamed.'

'All our knowledge is but the knowledge of school-children. Possibly we shall know a little more than we do now. But the real nature of things, that we shall never know, never.'

The magic of science, as portrayed by Joseph Wright of Derby in his painting The Orrery

Intellectual work

Einstein would not be happy in a modern scientific research department where collaboration on vast projects is the norm. His was a solitary quest, lit from within by flashes of inspiration. Strokes of genius rarely come from teamwork, even though a dedicated team may be needed afterwards to transform the insight into formal proofs or practical applications.

Einstein in his study at Princeton University

'The years of anxious searching in the dark for a truth that one feels but cannot express, the intense desire and the alternations of confidence and misgiving until one achieves clarity and understanding, can be understood only by those who have experienced them.'

'Whether it be a work of art or a significant scientific achievement, that which is great and noble comes from the solitary personality. European culture made its most important break away from stifling stagnation when the Renaissance offered the individual the possibility of unfettered development.'

'One should not pursue goals that are easily achieved. One must develop an instinct for what one can just barely achieve through one's greatest efforts.'

Disdaining fame

Einstein was not impressed by his own fame any more than by that of others. He tucked most awards and letters of praise away in a corner of his office which he called the 'boasting corner'. The only one which did make it into a frame and on to his wall was his diploma from the Bern Scientific Society, which he received in 1936.

'Everything that has anything to do with the cult of personality has always been painful to me.'

Einstein the public figure, with wife Elsa, greets the crowds at Pasadena, 1931

Einstein in New York, 1932

'One perceived that the hierarchies of the earth, in spite of his high place among them, were invisible to him, he held the stuff of life towards the light in some way so that that kind of embroidery did not show.'

[Rebecca West, 1931]

Courage in adversity

E INSTEIN suffered much during his life. There were personal
tragedies, such as the failure of his marriage to Mileva, the
probable death of his daughter Lieserl, his estrangement from his
children, his son Eduard's mental illness and the deaths of his
beloved mother and his wife Elsa. He was caught up in the anti-
Semitism that was rife in Europe in the 1920s and 1930s and was

driven out of Germany by the Nazis. He witnessed many of his fellow scientists and friends being persecuted and driven from their homeland and he saw many of them die in advance of him. He gave poignant advice to some of his friends and correspondents as they, too, suffered hardships. His counsel came in the form of an insight into how he bore his own difficulties.

'Read no newspapers, try to find a few friends who think as you do, read the wonderful writers of earlier times, Kant, Goethe, Lessing, and the classics of other lands, and enjoy the natural beauties of Munich's surroundings. Make believe all the time that you are living, so to speak, on Mars among alien creatures and blot out any deeper interest in the actions of those creatures. Make friends with a few animals. Then you will become a cheerful man once more and nothing will be able to trouble you.'

Opposite: *Nazi stormtroopers organize a boycott of Jewish businesses, 1933*

Growing older

I live in that solitude which is painful
in youth, but delicious in the years of
maturity.'

'I have become a lonely old fellow. A kind
of patriarchal figure who is displayed on
various occasions as an oddity. But in my
work I am more fanatical than ever and I
really entertain the hope that I have
solved my old problems of the unity of
the physical field. It is, however, like
being in an airship in which one can
cruise around in the clouds but cannot
see clearly how one can return to reality,
i.e. to earth.'

'Anything really new is invented only in one's youth. Later one becomes more experienced, more famous — and more stupid.'

'I've reached an age when, if somebody tells me to wear socks, I don't have to.'

Growing old cheerfully: Einstein at a Princeton luncheon, 1953

Into the unknown

I T was clear to Einstein that much would be written about him after his death, as it had been in his life. He knew that a lot of it would be unjust or even untrue. His solace was that his real, meaningful contribution was to physics and could not be misrepresented. Of the rest, it was out of his hands.

'There have already been published by the bucketful such brazen lies and utter fictions about me that I would long since have gone to my grave if I had let myself pay attention to them. One must console oneself with the thought that Time has a sieve through which most of these important things run into the ocean of oblivion.'

On a boating holiday, 1945

'Dear Posterity
If you have not become more just, more
peaceful, and generally more rational
than we are (or were) — why, then the
Devil take you.'

Encroaching death

MANY of Einstein's dearest friends died before him, and he wrote eloquently of their passing.

'In quitting this strange world he [Michelangelo Besso] has once again preceded me by a little. That doesn't mean anything. For those of us who believe in physics, the separation between past, present and future is only an illusion, however tenacious.'

His own encroaching death held no fear for him.

'I have firmly resolved to bite the dust, when my time comes, with a minimum of medical assistance, and up to then I will sin to my wicked heart's content.'

'I feel myself so much a part of everything living that I am not the least concerned with the beginning or ending of the concrete existence of any one person in this eternal flow.'

'It is tasteless to prolong life artificially. I have done my share; it is time to go. I will do it elegantly.'

Einstein shows his carefree side; below: *report of his death,* New York World-Telegram

Last words

EINSTEIN'S last words are not recorded. They were spoken in German, and the nurse in the room did not understand the language. So the last words should go to others who knew him well.

Elsa Einstein summed up his genius in a throwaway remark she made at the Mount Wilson Observatory in California. An astronomer showed her a new telescope and explained that it was used for finding out the shape of the universe. Elsa responded:

Einstein arrives in his new home, America, 4 April, 1921

'Oh, my husband does that on the back of an old envelope!'

And finally, Cornelius Lanczos wrote on Einstein's death:

'One feels that such a man lives forever, in the sense that a man like Beethoven can never die. But there is something forever lost: his sheer joy of living, which was so much a part of his being. It is hard to realize that this man, so unbelievably modest and unassuming, abides with us here no longer. He was aware of the unique role that Fate had bestowed on him, and aware, too, of his greatness. But precisely because this greatness was so towering, it made him modest and humble — not as a pose but as an inner necessity.'

WHO'S WHO

Michelangelo Besso, 1873–1955
Mathematician and close, life-long friend of Einstein

Sir James Chadwick, 1891–1974
British physicist who discovered the neutron and, with Ernest Rutherford, the proton. He won the Nobel Prize for Physics in 1935.

John Douglas Cockroft (1897–1967) and
Ernest Thomas Sinton Walton (1903–1995)
Built the first particle accelerator and broke apart the nucleus of a lithium atom using accelerated protons at the Cavendish Laboratory, Cambridge in 1932. They jointly won the Nobel Prize for Physics in 1951.

Nicolaus Copernicus (Nikolaj Kopernik), 1473–1543
Polish astronomer who proposed that the Earth is not the centre of the universe but revolves around the sun.

Marie Curie (Maria Sklodowska), 1867-1934
Polish-born chemist who, with her husband Pierre Curie, worked on radioactivity discovering alpha, beta and gamma types and the elements polonium and radium. The couple shared the Nobel Prize for Physics with Henri Becquerel in 1903, making Marie the first woman to win a Nobel Prize.

René Descartes, 1596–1650
French philosopher who strove to establish a solid base for knowledge. Descartes also developed a system of calculus.

Helen Dukas, 1896–1982
Personal secretary of Albert Einstein from 1928 until his death. She was also his housekeeper after Elsa's death in 1936.

Friedrich Dürrenmatt, 1921–1990
Swiss dramatist whose plays include *The Physicists*, in which one character believes himself to be Einstein and another believes he is Newton but pretends to be Einstein.

Sir Frank Watson Dyson, 1868–1939

Astronomer Royal in the UK, 1910–1933. He oversaw the introduction of more accurate clocks at the Greenwich Observatory, where GMT was kept for the world.

Sir Arthur Stanley Eddington, 1882–1944

Astrophysicist who investigated the movement, internal structure and evolution of stars.

Euclid (Eukleides), *fl.* c300 BCE

Classical Greek mathematician who taught at Alexandria, Egypt. He set out the foundations of geometry in the *Elements*.

Enrico Fermi, 1902–1954

Italian-born physicist who discovered neutron-induced radioactivity and, with Leo Szilard, produced the first controlled nuclear chain reaction.

Galileo Galilei, 1564–1642

Italian philosopher, scientist and mathematician who revolutionized the study of motion with his discoveries about the behaviour of falling bodies, inertia and parabolic trajectories.

Carl Friedrich Gauss, 1777–1855

One of the west's greatest mathematicians; he developed a way of measuring curvature and challenged Euclid's geometry.

Conrad Habicht, 1884–1948

Close friend of Einstein. Einstein, Habicht and Maurice Solovine formed the Akademie Olympia, a group for the three of them to discuss texts on science and philosophy as well as their own work in Bern, 1902–1904.

Werner Heisenberg, 1901–1976

German physicist who proposed the uncertainty (or indeterminacy) principle in 1927. He won the Nobel Prize for Physics in 1932.

Banesh Hoffman, 1906–1986

A student of Einstein's and later a close colleague.

Edwin Powell Hubble, 1889–1953

American astronomer who provided the first evidence of the expansion of the universe.

Christiaan Huygens, 1629–1695

Dutch mathematician, physicist and astronomer who formulated the wave theory of light.

Leopold Infeld, 1889–1968
Polish physicist who worked with Einstein in Princeton in the 1930s. With Einstein, he formulated the equation describing the movement of stars.

Georges Lemaître, 1894–1966
Belgian astronomer who formulated the Big Bang theory to explain the origin of the universe.

Hendrik Antoon Lorentz, 1853–1928
Dutch physicist who, with Pieter Zeeman, won the Nobel Prize for Physics in 1902 for the theory of electromagnetic radiation. He suggested that atoms are made up of charged particles.

James Clerk Maxwell, 1831–1879
Scottish physicist who first observed the constant speed of light, formulated the electromagnetic theory and his field equations which describe the fundamentals of electricity and magnetism.

John Michell, 1724–1793
English astronomer and geologist who first suggested the possibility of stars so dense that light cannot escape from them (now known as black holes).

Hermann Minkowski, 1864–1909
German mathematician born in Russia who developed the idea of combining three-dimensional space with time as a fourth dimension.

Isaac Newton, 1642–1727
English mathematician and physicist whose three laws of motion form the basis of modern physics. He discovered the spectrum of colours that make up white light, developed differential calculus and formulated the general theory of gravitation.

J. Robert Oppenheimer, 1904–1967
American physicist; founder and director of the Los Alamos laboratory, the home of the Manhattan Project to develop nuclear weapons.

Max Planck, 1858–1947
German physicist, originator of quantum theory. He won the Nobel Prize for Physics in 1918.

Bernhard Riemann, 1826–1866
German mathematician who developed the mathematics that formed the basis of Einstein's model of four-dimensional space-time.

Franklin D. Roosevelt, 1882–1945
President of the United States during the Second World War, who set up the Manhattan Project to develop nuclear weapons.

Bertrand Russell (Earl Russell), 1872–1970
British philosopher, social reformer and peace activist. He won the Nobel Prize for Literature in 1950.

Ernest Rutherford (Baron Rutherford), 1871–1937
British physicist generally considered the principal founder of atomic physics; he developed the nuclear theory of atomic structure. He won the Nobel Prize for Chemistry in 1908.

Erwin Schrödinger, 1887–1961
Austrian physicist who helped to develop the theory that particles of matter may in some circumstances behave like waves. He shared the Nobel Prize for Physics with P. A. M. Dirac in 1933.

Karl Schwarzschild, 1873–1916
German astronomer who used Einstein's equations to formulate a theory of black holes.

Benedict de Spinoza, 1632–1677
Dutch-Jewish philosopher who was the foremost proponent of Rationalism of his time.

Leo Szilard, 1898–1964
Hungarian-born physicist who was instrumental in starting the Manhattan Project to develop nuclear weapons. With Enrico Fermi he produced the first controlled chain reaction from nuclear fission.

Rabindranath Tagore, 1861–1941
Bengali writer who introduced new verse forms into Bengali poetry, freeing it from the traditional forms based on the models of classical Sanskrit. He won the Nobel Prize for Literature in 1913.

William Thomson (Baron Kelvin), 1824–1907
Scottish engineer, mathematician and physicist who proposed the electromagnetic theory of light.

Chaim Weizmann, 1874–1952
President of the World Zionist Organization from 1920 and first president of Israel.

Text Credits

Einstein's original text is © Hebrew University and Princeton University Press, and is here reprinted by permission of the Albert Einstein Archives, Hebrew University of Jerusalem.

In addition, material on pp. 7, 12, 27, 28 has been taken from *Einstein Lived Here*, Albert Pais (1994) and is here reproduced by kind permission of Oxford University Press.

Image credits

Art Archive: 26, 106, 124, 134

Corbis: 7, 8, 12, 14, 20, 24, 28, 31, 33, 34, 37, 39, 53, 61, 70, 75, 79, 85, 87, 91 (both), 95, 100, 103, 105, 110, 112, 118, 121, 127, 128, 131, 133, 136, 139, 141, 145, 151, 155, 157, 159, 176, 178, 183, 185 (both), 186

Getty Images: 11, 23, 40, 43, 44, 50, 92, 99, 117, 143, 164, 167, 174, 177, 181

Getty Images/AFP: 67, 152, 168, 171

Getty Images/Time Life: 69, 147

Kobal Collection: 59

Rex Features: 19

Shutterstock Images: 49, 54, 56, 63, 64, 72, 80, 109, 115, 123, 148, 161, 163

Science Photo Library: 46, 77, 82

Topham Picturepoint: 16